HIDEOUS HISTORY

DREADFUL DISASTERS

by William Anthony

BEARPORT
PUBLISHING

Minneapolis, Minnesota

Credits

Images are courtesy of Shutterstock.com. With thanks to Getty Images, Thinkstock Photo, and iStockphoto. Front Cover – Everett Collection, Vadim Sadovski. 4–5 – PhotoJuli86, Romolo Tavani, KingVector, johavel. 6–7 – solarseven, Eva Kali, Herschel Hoffmeyer, Kakigori Studio. 8–9 – Everett Collection, Meganom. 10–11 – Rolf E. Staerk, Naypong Studio, elena castaldi viora, Steve Heap. 12–13 – Ben Gingell, Antoine Buchet, Miraphoto, Gaidamashchuk. 14–15 – Multigon. 16–17 – Dotted Yeti, Standret, Daniel Eskridge, Peyker, NYgraphic. 18–19 – Mo Wu, Yanfei Sun, baldezh. 20–21 – M. Rinandar Tasya, Masi Perez, Sabelskaya. 22–23 – ivanoel, Protasov AN, ianakauri. 24–25 – Alican Ozkeskin, BlackMac, Marcin Babul. 26–27 – Vagabjorn, YegoroV, Mopic, Dolvalol. 28–29 – africa2008st, Supatsara Ratchanet, common human. 30 – Mgr. Nobody.

Bearport Publishing Company Product Development Team

President: Jen Jenson; Director of Product Development: Spencer Brinker; Managing Editor: Allison Juda; Associate Editor: Naomi Reich; Associate Editor: Tiana Tran; Senior Designer: Colin O'Dea; Associate Designer: Elena Klinkner; Associate Designer: Kayla Eggert; Product Development Specialist: Anita Stasson

Library of Congress Cataloging-in-Publication Data

Names: Anthony, William (Children's author), author.
Title: Dreadful disasters / by William Anthony.
Description: Minneapolis, Minnesota : Bearport Publishing Company, [2024] |
  Series: Hideous history | Includes bibliographical references and index.
Identifiers: LCCN 2023010549 (print) | LCCN 2023010550 (ebook) | ISBN
  9798888220276 (library binding) | ISBN 9798888222171 (paperback) | ISBN
  9798888223420 (ebook)
Subjects: LCSH: Disasters--History--Juvenile literature.
Classification: LCC D24 .A64 2024 (print) | LCC D24 (ebook) | DDC
  904--dc23/eng/20230307
LC record available at https://lccn.loc.gov/2023010549
LC ebook record available at https://lccn.loc.gov/2023010550

For more information, write to Bearport Publishing, 5357 Penn Avenue South, Minneapolis, MN 55419.

CONTENTS

Pieces of the Past 4

Dinosaur Disaster 6

The Partying Prince 8

Changing Minds 10

London Is Burning 12

Iceberg Incident 14

The Rise of the Humans 16

Bursting Banks. 18

Cloudy with a Chance of Cloud . . 20

Swarm. 22

Frozen in Time. 24

The Split 26

The Eight-Month Eruption 28

Hideous History 30

Glossary 31

Index 32

Read More 32

Learn More Online 32

PIECES OF THE PAST

There are secrets everywhere. You just need to know where to look. Bodies, books, and buildings are all buried below the ground you walk on.

The past was hard for those who had to live through it.

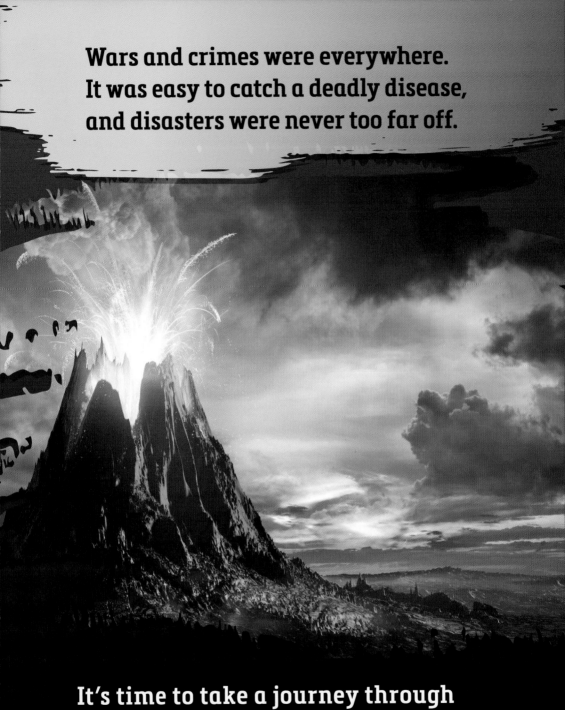

Wars and crimes were everywhere.
It was easy to catch a deadly disease,
and disasters were never too far off.

It's time to take a journey through
the past. Are you properly prepared
to learn about the hideous history
of horrific disasters?

DINOSAUR DISASTER

Dinosaurs had jaws that could have ripped a car in half. Yet, the disaster that wiped them off the planet was even scarier than they were.

How did it happen? Some scientists think an **asteroid** hit Earth around 65 million years ago. They say it sent lots of dust flying into the air.

Other scientists think huge volcanoes **erupted** and filled the air with ash.

Whether from an asteroid or a volcanic eruption, all the dust in the air blocked out sunlight. Earth got cold, and plants died.

Then, it got very hot. Animals, including dinosaurs, were the next to go.

THE PARTYING PRINCE

England's King Henry I had only one **heir** to his throne. It was Prince William Adelin. Unfortunately, disaster struck before Prince William got to take the throne.

Prince William went to battle. When it was time to come home, the prince boarded a boat named the *White Ship*.

The ship never made it back to England. On the way, it struck a rock. William and his crew were too busy partying to notice.

The ship sank with hundreds of people on board. Only a single person survived.

CHANGING MINDS

Most disasters destroy things and cost people lots of money. Some disasters change how people think.

On November 1, 1755, lots of Christians in Lisbon, Portugal, were in church. Suddenly, the ground began to shake.

One of the biggest earthquakes in Europe's history hit Lisbon!

Buildings fell down, and many people were crushed. Lots of people blamed God.

But soon, some began to think the disaster had something to do with our planet instead. It was one of the first times the people there tried to explain a disaster using science.

LONDON IS BURNING

Sometimes, humans can cause the biggest disasters. In 1666, one baker accidentally started a fire that took over London, England.

Thomas Farriner owned a bakery on Pudding Lane. One night, a spark from his oven started a fire in the bakery. There had been no rain, so his wooden building was very dry.

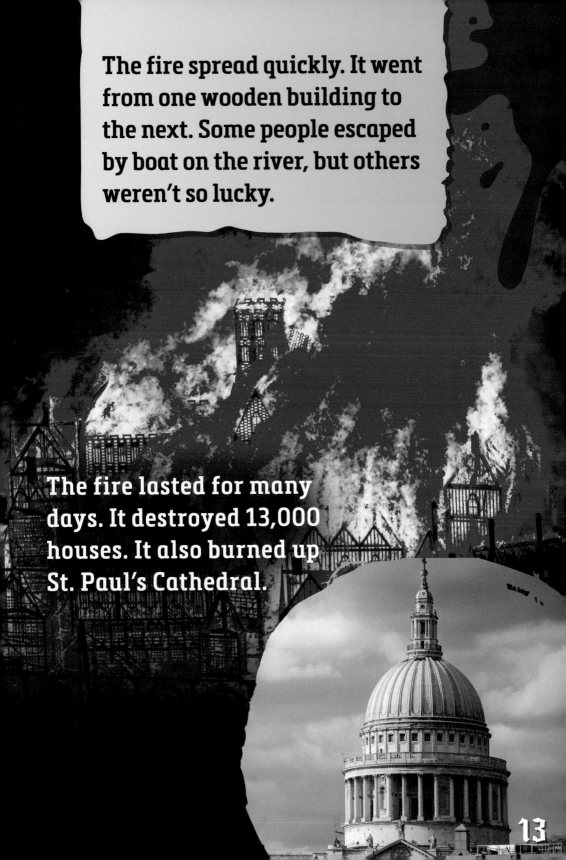

The fire spread quickly. It went from one wooden building to the next. Some people escaped by boat on the river, but others weren't so lucky.

The fire lasted for many days. It destroyed 13,000 houses. It also burned up St. Paul's Cathedral.

ICEBERG INCIDENT

People were very **confident** when they set sail on the *Titanic*. It was a very big ship for the time. People thought it was unsinkable.

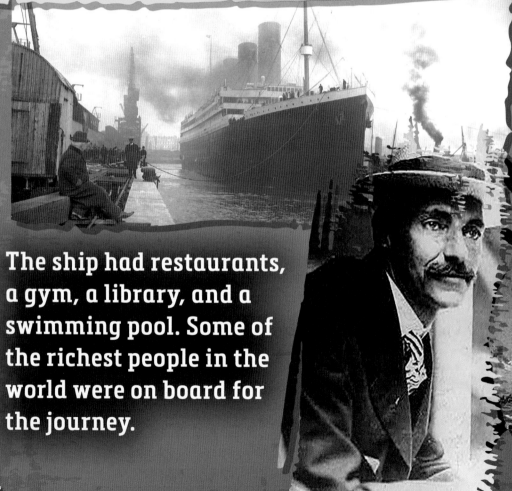

The ship had restaurants, a gym, a library, and a swimming pool. Some of the richest people in the world were on board for the journey.

The *Titanic* set sail for New York in April 1912. One night, the ship was going through icy waters.

It hit a big iceberg. The *Titanic* was damaged and began to sink. More than 1,500 people died on that fateful night.

THE RISE OF THE HUMANS

Earth is always changing temperature. It can be very hot for millions of years. Then, it can turn very cold for millions more. The coldest periods are called ice ages.

When ice covers more of the world than usual, it can spell disaster for some. Many animals and plants can't **adapt** to the cold quickly enough.

Many living things died during the last ice age. Others, such as woolly mammoths and saber-toothed tigers, were able to survive.

Humans were able to adapt quickly to the cold. When the world started to get warm again, humans survived this, too.

BURSTING BANKS

Disasters are often measured by how many people died. There is nothing nice about it, but that's hideous history for you. One of the deadliest disasters happened in China.

The second-longest river in China is called the Yellow River. It floods often. However, one flood in 1887 was much worse than normal.

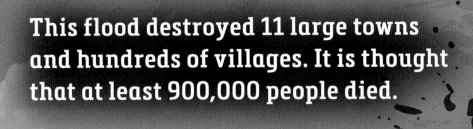

This flood destroyed 11 large towns and hundreds of villages. It is thought that at least 900,000 people died.

The people who survived had climbed on houses and trees to get out of the water's path. When the flood was over, there was a lot of rebuilding to do.

CLOUDY WITH A CHANCE OF CLOUD

The summer of 1816 was not like other summers. It was very cold and there was snow. Plants did not grow well. This was all due to a giant volcano.

Mount Tambora is a volcano in Indonesia. It erupted twice in 1815. The second time, it could be heard hundreds of miles away.

It was the biggest explosion ever on Earth. Smoke and ash filled the sky. The volcano sent a kind of fog around the planet.

The fog blocked sunlight. That summer was much colder because the sun couldn't warm Earth up!

SWARM

A little grasshopper might not look like it could cause a disaster. But you'd be surprised!

Locusts have long been a big problem for farmers all over the world. The insects fly around eating crops and other plants. People in North America found out just how much of a problem they were in 1875.

Millions of locusts gathered together in groups called swarms. There were so many they looked like huge clouds.

They ate thousands of plants. Many people did not have food because locusts ate all the crops on farms!

FROZEN IN TIME

In Italy, there is a city where an extreme disaster is frozen in time. Its name is Pompeii.

Statues still stand tall. Furniture hasn't moved for almost 2,000 years. You can see **casts** of people moments before they died all those years ago. But how?

Pompeii was a busy city near the volcano Mount Vesuvius. In 79 CE, the volcano erupted. It created a cloud of ash and smoke more than 20 miles (30 km) high.

Lava and ash quickly covered the city and its people. Then, the lava hardened, keeping everything perfectly in place. We can still see those things today!

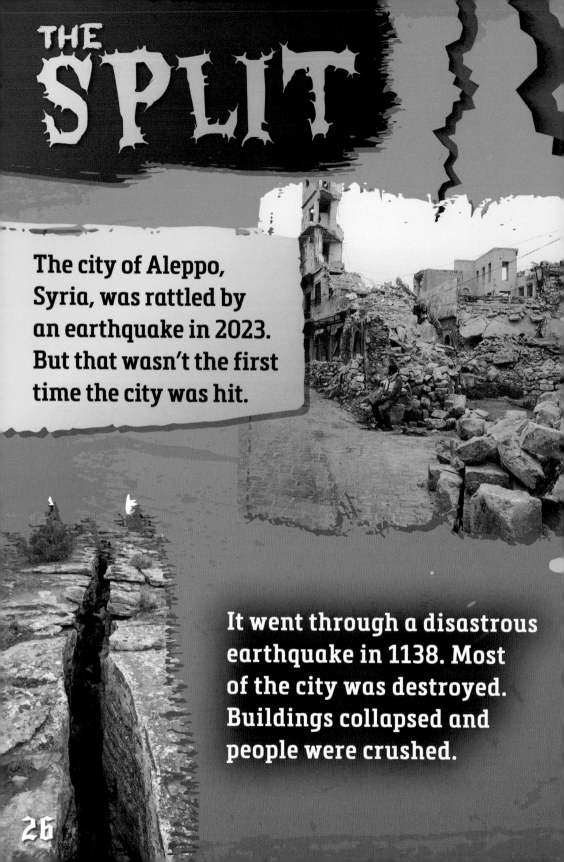

THE SPLIT

The city of Aleppo, Syria, was rattled by an earthquake in 2023. But that wasn't the first time the city was hit.

It went through a disastrous earthquake in 1138. Most of the city was destroyed. Buildings collapsed and people were crushed.

Aleppo has a history of earthquakes thanks to **what's going on below Earth's surface.** The city sits where two **tectonic plates** meet.

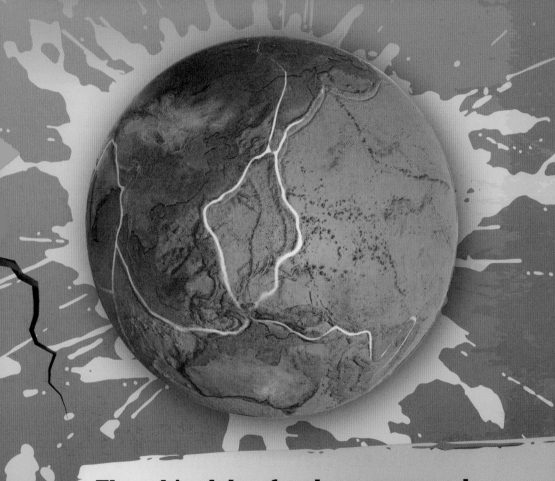

These big slabs of rock move around slowly and bump into each other. This can make earthquakes happen.

THE EIGHT-MONTH ERUPTION

Laki is a group of volcanoes in Iceland. In 1783, they exploded in one of the biggest eruptions in recent history. It lasted for eight months!

The volcanoes let out lots of things during those months. One of them was sulphur. This dangerous gas became part of the air.

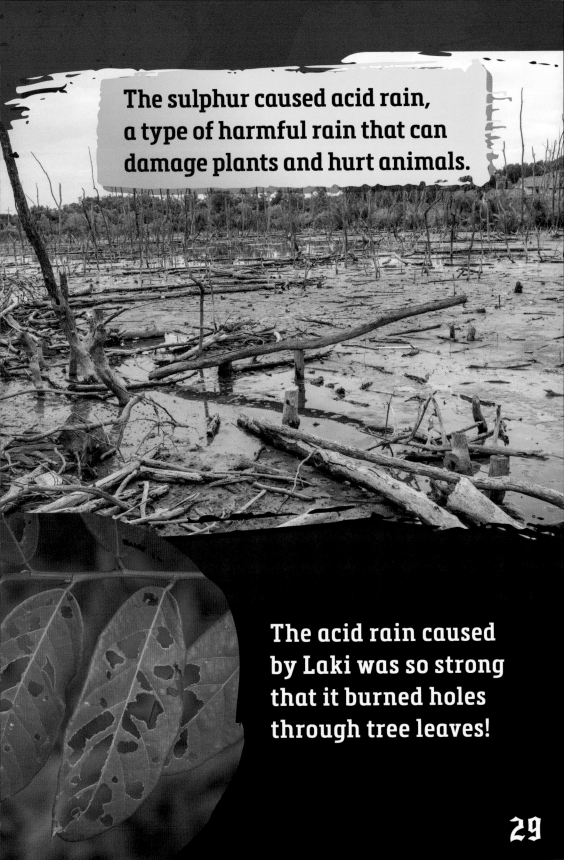

The sulphur caused acid rain, a type of harmful rain that can damage plants and hurt animals.

The acid rain caused by Laki was so strong that it burned holes through tree leaves!

HIDEOUS HISTORY

You can relax now. Let your heart calm down. The past was a terrifying place, but you do not live there.

These stories just go to show that the past was full of disasters.

GLOSSARY

adapt to change over a long period of time

asteroid a very large rock from space

casts objects created by a material hardening over or in something else

confident having a strong belief in something's ability

erupted sent out lava, ash, steam, and gas from a volcano

heir someone who will take over or receive something, such as a title

tectonic plates massive slabs of rock that make up Earth's surface

INDEX

acid rain 29

asteroid 6–7

earthquakes 10, 26–27

fire 12–13

flood 18–19

ice age 16–17

locusts 22–23

ships 8–9, 14–15

tectonic plates 27

volcanoes 7, 20–21, 25, 28

READ MORE

Hamen, Susan E. *The 12 Worst Earthquakes of All Time (All-Time Worst Disasters).* Mankato, MN: 12–Story Library, 2019.

Regan, Lisa. *Disasters (Fact Frenzy: Planet Earth).* New York: PowerKids Press, 2020.

Wallace, Elise. *Failure: Disasters in History.* Huntington Beach, CA: Teacher Created Materials, 2019.

LEARN MORE ONLINE

1. Go to **www.factsurfer.com** or scan the QR code below.

2. Enter "**Dreadful Disasters**" into the search box.

3. Click on the cover of this book to see a list of websites.